Lillian Too

Lillian Too

ELEMENT

Shaftesbury, Dorset • Boston, Massachusetts
Melbourne, Victoria

© Element Books 1998

Text © Lillian Too 1998

First published in the UK in 1998 by
Element Books Limited
Shaftesbury, Dorset SP7 8BP

Published in the USA in 1998 by
Element Books, Inc.
160 North Washington Street, Boston MA 02114

Published in Australia in 1998 by
Element Books
and distributed by Penguin Australia Limited
487 Maroondah Highway, Ringwood, Victoria 3134

First Impression October 1998
Reprinted October and November (twice) 1998
Reprinted December 1998 (twice)
Reprinted 1999

Lillian Too's moral right as the author of this book has been asserted.

Cover design by Mark Slader based on
a concept by The Bridgewater Book Company
Design and Typesetting by Drum Enterprises Limited
Printed and bound in Great Britain by Bemrose Security Printing, Derby

British Library Cataloguing in Publication
data available

Library of Congress Cataloging in Publication
data available

ISBN 1 86204 514 3

This little gem of a book is dedicated with big love to my daughter Jennifer.

INTRODUCTION

The tips in this little book will transform your life by harnessing the positive energy of your environment. Use them to arrange your home and work place so as to accumulate auspicious energy for happiness, prosperity and good health. As well as advice on lucky symbols and features, colours and room layouts, there are warnings of what to avoid and tips on how to deflect and dissolve inauspicious energy lines.

Lillian Too

UNDERSTANDING THE FLOW OF CHI

Feng shui is understanding the flow of chi, the hidden life breath that permeates the environment. When chi is in disarray, misfortunes rule the day. Learn to recognize the hidden energies of chi.

YIN AND YANG IN THE COSMIC BALANCE

All the energies of your personal space are in a constant state of flux. Yin and yang energies dance together continually – striving for the cosmic balance that brings harmony. Yin is cool and dark and lifeless. Yang is hot and bright and full of life. Keep these forces in harmony within your home and you will enjoy good luck.

YANG ENERGY
FOR SUCCESS

Create yin and yang balance with
comfortable levels of light and shade ... and
for success add slightly more light to
emphasize and enhance your yang energy.

REGULAR SHAPES
ARE BETTER

Regular shapes are to be preferred to
irregular shapes. Squares and rectangles have
better feng shui than triangles or shapes
with missing corners.

Ratio Of Windows

The ratio of windows to doors in all your rooms should not exceed 3:1. Too many windows cause all your luck to seep away. It is also better not to have windows on the wall opposite the door.

WINDCHIMES IN THE NORTHWEST

Windchimes work best when placed in the northwest. A six-rod windchime here attracts mentors and influential people into your life. It also assists the family patriarch's luck.

DISPLAY THE THREE-LEGGED FROG FOR LUCK

Look for a three-legged frog – you can buy one from any Chinese supermarket – and place it in the vicinity of your front door, facing inwards as if it has just come into the house. Don't place the frog facing the door.

WATER FEATURES WORK BEST IN THE NORTH

Mini water fountains and small ponds in your garden bring exceptional money luck when located in the north or southeast corners.

BEWARE OF STRAIGHT ROADS

Don't let the front of your house, especially the front door, face an oncoming straight road or your house will be attacked by 'tigers in the night'. Block the negative energy coming toward you with a clump of trees, a fence, a wall, a hedge or a Pa Kua symbol.

CURVED PATHWAYS BRING BETTER LUCK

Any pathway that leads to your front door should meander, thereby slowing down the chi or cosmic energy that brings good fortune.

BRING IN
FRESH AIR

At least once a week, open two windows in two different rooms to let fresh air sweep away any stale yin air in your rooms. It is a good idea to do this on a sunny day to bring in vibrant yang energy which attracts good fortune.

Fresh Flowers
For More Yang

Fresh flowers bring precocious yang energy
into the living rooms and halls of your
home, but they become depressingly yin
when they wither and die. Never leave dying
flowers in your home. Replace them with
fresh ones immediately.

USING ARTIFICIAL FLOWERS

You can find fabulous artificial flowers – silk or even plastic – which are infinitely preferable to dried flowers. If you have dried plants in your home your chances of success will be serious undermined. Never display dried flowers. Feng shui does not consider them auspicious.

BALANCING THE YANG OF SUMMER AND THE YIN OF WINTER

Yang reigns supreme in the summer months so introduce a little bit of yin in the form of water to establish cosmic balance and bring good fortune. In the winter when yin reigns, the yang of fire brings warmth and light to dreary days.

SUPPORT FROM BEHIND

Tap the protective energies of strong and solid features such as hills or a large, tall structure by making certain they are at the back of your home. When there are trees or higher ground behind your home, you will enjoy the protection of the celestial turtle. When the higher ground is in front of your home, you are said to be confronting an immovable obstacle.

WATER SHOULD BE
ON THE LEFT

Any water feature in front of the house
should be located on the left of the main
door from inside the house looking out. This
will ensure the stability of married couples
living there. Water on the right-hand side
causes husbands to have a roving eye.

UNDULATING LAND IS EXCELLENT FENG SHUI

Feng shui teaches you to use your environment wisely. If your land and the surrounding area is undulating it is said to house auspicious dragons. When land is flat and featureless, the dragon is missing and the land is said to be less auspicious.

GENTLE SLOPES ARE LUCKIER THAN CRAGGY SLOPES

Broad contours and undulating inclines are always preferred to excessively steep and craggy slopes. When the elevations are gentle, chi turns benign and prosperous; it moves slowly, accumulating and settling and bringing great good fortune.

MIDLEVELS ARE SUPERIOR TO THE PEAKS

Living at the very top of hills and mountains is not auspicious. On the top of a hill you will be exposed to strong winds; lower down the hill, in its gentle embrace, you will be sheltered from the elements.

MEANDERING WATER
BRINGS MONEY

When water meanders slowly in the direction of your house, you will prosper effortlessly. Straight, fast-moving rivers carry water away from you without allowing good fortune to collect.

WATERFALLS BRING MILLION-DOLLAR OPPORTUNITIES

When there is a view of a natural waterfall that appears to bring water to your home, you will definitely become rich. In the Far East countless people have become millionaires after introducing an artificial waterfall in to their gardens. But remember not to overdo it. Balance is vital – too much water can drown you!

PROTRUDING CORNERS CREATE 'KNIFE EDGES'

Soften the sharp, harmful edges of square pillars or protruding corners by placing a plant directly in front of them. This deflects and dissolves all the killing energy released by the edge. Change the plant regularly since it cannot survive the killing chi coming from the corner.

DEFLECT THE KILLING ENERGY OF OVERHEAD BEAMS

Exposed overhead beams cause bad energy to press down on anyone sitting or sleeping below. Hang a five-rod windchime on the beam to counter this feng shui defect in the home or office. Do ensure that the rods are hollow rather than solid so that the chi can travel through them and transform into good luck.

USE MIRRORS TO ENLARGE TIGHT CORNERS

Large mirrors are excellent for enhancing the stale energy of a tight or cramped space. This is especially recommended for tiny halls or foyers. Place the mirror on a wall that does not face the door. Let the mirror create a feeling of space but do not let it reflect the door directly since this will cause all the good fortune to dissipate.

Trees Are A Valuable Asset

Plants and trees around a home are deemed to be auspicious because the 'wood' element signifies growth and development. They are particularly lucky when allowed to thrive in the east, the southeast and the south. Trees should be pruned regularly and not allowed to overwhelm the house.

KEEP A PET

Pets are especially good feng shui in homes that are left empty during the day. If the family are out working or at school, yin energy accumulates in the silence and stillness. This can be countered by the lively presence of a dog or cat or fish.

Try The Turtle Exercise

You can do this gentle, calming exercise sitting or standing, with your eyes open or closed. Relax and drop your chin on to your chest. Breathe in and at the same time, slowly raise your head until you are looking forward. Tilt your head further back until you are looking upward, simultaneously exhaling. Repeat this eight times.

HANG A PICTURE OF A SUNRISE IN THE SOUTH

The south is the place of new opportunities, the location of the crimson phoenix. A picture of a sunrise in this corner of your living room will open up bright new avenues for growth in your life.

KEEP A TANK FULL OF FISH TO LIFT YOUR CAREER

In feng shui tradition fish always bring good luck. Place a tank of lively guppies in the north corner of your living room and watch your career come alive with positive new developments.

Choose Armchairs And Sofas That Support

Your sofas and chairs should have generous back support and comfortable arm rests. Arrange them to form a square, with a footstool to complete the symbolism of perfect feng shui. Avoid L-shaped arrangements – they are less auspicious.

A SOUTHERN FIREPLACE

If you have a fireplace in your living room the best place for it is on the south wall, but it is also auspicious in the east, southeast, southwest and northeast. The northwest is not a good place for a fireplace. If you have one here, consider closing it up or simply not using it.

MAIN DOORS SHOULD OPEN INTO 'BRIGHT HALLS'

When your main door opens onto a wide open space, like a park or playground, and into a large hall or living room, it is known as the bright hall effect. An open, uncramped area allows beneficial chi to accumulate.

MAIN DOOR TABOOS

The main door is the 'mouth' of the house. Its feng shui affects the entire household, so it should be sited carefully. If possible, ensure that it is:

- Not facing a toilet, staircase or mirror

- Not facing a pillar, the edge of two walls, or a protruding corner

- Not below a toilet on the floor above

PAINT YOUR
FRONT DOOR

Create feng shui harmony by painting your front door according to the element of the direction it faces:

- Red for south, soutwest or northeast
- Blue for north, east or southeast
- White for west, northwest or north
- Green for east, southeast or south

ACTIVATE THE WEALTH CORNER OF YOUR LIVING ROOM

The Universal Wealth corner is the southeast. Energize this corner by placing a leafy green plant or a bubbling aquarium there. But do this only in the living room, not in bedrooms, toilets or the dining room.

ENHANCE YOUR SOCIAL LIFE WITH FENG SHUI

Hang a bright light and place a cluster of natural quartz crystals in the southwest corner of your home, your living room or bedroom. The light should be turned on for at least three hours each evening. This will transform your social life – but be patient, feng shui takes time to work.

FIND A PARTNER

If you are fed up with being single, energize your southwest corner by placing a 5-foot-high floor light there to tap the energy of the earth. Keep the light turned on every evening until you achieve your goal. But don't use this tip unless you want to find a partner!

ACTIVATE ROMANCE LUCK WITH MANDARIN DUCKS

Keep a painting or a pair of ornamental mandarin ducks on a table in the southwest corner of your bedroom to enhance romance and luck. Ducks symbolize fidelity and happiness. An alternative would be anything heart shaped.

FENG SHUI IN THE BEDROOM

- Never allow mirrors to reflect the bed. Reflections in the mirror suggest the presence of a third party.

- Do not sleep under an exposed beam. This causes sleepless nights and a rift between couples. Camouflage any beams with fake ceilings or hang two bamboo stems tied with red thread.

POSITIONING BEDS FOR
GOOD LUCK

Always place your bed in the corner of the
bedroom diagonally opposite the entrance.
Never sleep with your head or feet pointing
directly at the door.

BEDROOM DOORS

- The door into your bedroom should not
  face a kitchen or toilet door. Hang a
  windchime between the two doors to
  dissolve the bad energy created.

- Bedroom doors should not face a
  staircase, a mirror or another door. If
  they do, keep them closed or hang a light
  or windchime. Do not use a Pa Kua
  mirror – these should only be used
  outside the home.

SLEEPING

- Always have a bed head.
- Push the head of your bed against the wall.
- Sleep at least 18 ins/45 cm above the floor.
- Never sleep facing away from the door – you should always be able to see the entrance.
- Keep lighting low and soft.
- Decorate with dark yin colours rather than light yang colours.

PAINTINGS IN THE BEDROOM

Do not hang pictures of fierce animals, abstract subjects or water in the bedroom. Elsewhere, water is very good feng shui, but in the bedroom it suggests financial loss.

SLEEPING UNDER WINDOWS OR A CEILING FAN

Avoid having your bed underneath a window since this will disturb the energies around you all through the night. Use blinds and heavy curtains to cover the window. Try not to sleep directly under a ceiling fan or a very bright light. This also causes the energies to become too active during the night.

SLEEPING NEXT TO
LARGE WINDOWS

When you sleep next to very large windows, or, worse, if the bedroom door is next to the window, the chi entering your room is much too powerful. Your sleep will be disturbed and your energies over-stimulated. The result will be disharmony and discord. Cover the window with heavy drapes, or at least have a second lighter layer of curtains to diffuse the flow of chi.

SLEEPING BETWEEN
TWO DOORS

If your bed is located between the entrance
door and the door to the bathroom, the
energies that flow across your bed are said
to be afflicted. Rearrange your bed or place a
screen between the bed and one of the
doors.

BATHROOMS AND TOILETS

You may have heard that toilets are bad news wherever they are placed in the home. This is true, but do not fret since everyone has this problem! Keep the lid down on your toilets at all times and toilet doors permanently shut. Change the door hinges to ensure this, if necessary.

THE LOCATION OF TOILETS

If your toilet door directly faces the main door, install a very bright ceiling light between the two doors and keep it turned on to disperse bad chi and yin energy. A toilet in the southwest or centre of the house will affect family relationships. Install a bright light outside the toilet and keep the door closed at all times. Paint the door red, (very yang) to counter the yin energy of the toilet.

FLOWERS OR PLANTS LEFT IN THE TOILET

Toilets should be kept clean and neat but do not decorate them with plants, flowers, paintings or decorative objects. The reverse of what you hope for will happen. Filling the room with good luck symbols causes it to become a symbol of misfortune because its yin energy is so malignant and inauspicious.

DINING ROOMS AND FAMILY ROOMS

Dining rooms and family rooms should be the focus of a household. Fill them with yang energy:

- Paint the walls a bright, happy colour.

- Keep your stereo system or TV here to create noise and activity.

- Hang a wall mirror to reflect the food on the table or the happiness of the people.

FAMILY
PORTRAITS

Make an effort to photograph or paint a
family portrait with every member present.
Make sure everyone looks happy. Hang this
in the family room to symbolize a happy
family staying together forever. Put it on the
southwest wall if possible. If not, it should
face the south, southwest or northwest.

THE DIRECTION OF YOUR STAIRCASE

If your front door opens straight onto a staircase, negative energy rushes into the heart of the home. Block this off by placing a plant, a bright light, a windchime or a screen between the door and the staircase. Better still, turn the last three steps of the staircase so they no longer face the front door.

Staircase Construction

Staircases should curve gently from one floor to the next and be brightly lit to encourage chi to flow upstairs in a slow and meandering fashion. The steps should not have empty spaces between them since this causes good luck to seep away. Close up the spaces with solid wood to preserve the family's future.

BROAD STAIRCASES ARE MORE AUSPICIOUS

Homes with narrow staircases rarely house wealthy residents. Whether the staircase is straight or winding, when it is narrow, cramped and dark, the flow of energy can get blocked and the area becomes very yin. Correct this by changing your staircase altogether or use bright lights and solid balustrades to encourage chi to flow auspiciously upwards. Paint the staircase white and decorate with colourful paintings.

BEWARE OF THREE DOORS IN A ROW

This sort of configuration is a major feng shui taboo. If there are three doors in a row and one of them is the front door, the house is said to suffer from afflicted feng shui. One solution is to keep the middle door permanently closed. Otherwise use plants and furniture to create a barrier to slow down the flow of energy, or hang a windchime between the doors.

LONG CORRIDORS AND CRAMPED SPACES

If you have long, narrow corridors or cramped corners in your home, they should be painted white and kept well lit. This ensures that the good energies of the home do not become stagnant and turn into malignant and inauspicious energies that will harm the residents.

Rooms At The End Of A Long Corridor Tend To Be Unlucky

Bedrooms, studies or offices at the end of a long corridor are usually afflicted by killing energies that gather strength as they flow quickly down the narrow space. These energies represent the classical poison arrows of feng shui.

Counteract the effect by painting the door of the room:

- Red if it faces west or northwest
- Blue if it faces south
- White if it faces east or southeast
- Green if it faces southwest or northeast.

ENERGIZE HALLS AND FOYERS

Wood, fire and water are the elements that create good fortune. 'Water' gives life to the 'wood' which develops fruits in the warmth of the 'fire'. Keep your hall well lit and warm in winter, decorate it with plants and install a water feature – a small fountain or aquarium – for prosperity luck. Do the same thing in the reception areas of business premises.

WATER FEATURES

If you install a water feature with flowing water in a foyer or reception area to create prosperity luck, make certain that the water appears to be flowing *in* rather than *out*.

At The Office Sit With The Wall Behind You

If you want to have the support of your
superiors and colleagues, always sit with the
wall behind you and the door in front of
you. The wall provides security and
protection. To strengthen this support, hang
a picture of a mountain range behind you.
Remember, there is nothing stronger than a
mountain so why not use an image of the
Himalayas, the largest mountain range on
earth.

DO NOT SIT WITH YOUR BACK TO THE DOOR

Never sit with your back to the door. You are more likely to be cheated and betrayed and to lose in any office politicing. If you are presently sitting in such a way, rearrange your office and change your sitting position immediately.

DO NOT SIT WITH YOUR BACK TO A WINDOW OR BOOKCASE

If you sit with a window behind you, you will lack support. In any crisis or difficulty you will be among the first to suffer. Place a solid cabinet behind you to symbolize the mountain. But do not place a bookshelf there since this signifies knives cutting into your back. Open bookshelves should be closed up since they create hostile energies in the office.

THE BEST PLACE TO SIT IN AN OFFICE

The ideal sitting orientation is diagonal to the door, facing it. Desks should not face the door directly since the incoming energy will be too powerful. It is a good idea to have a light directly above the door to create auspicious yang energy in the office.

PLANTS IN THE OFFICE FOR AUSPICIOUS ENERGY FLOWS

Plants in the office are one of the most effective feng shui energizers. This is because they are of the wood element, signifying growth. Artificial plants are as effective as the real thing, but dried plants are not encouraged. Place the plants in the east, southeast or south corners of your office for maximum feng shui effect.

REPLACE DEFECTIVE LIGHT BULBS IMMEDIATELY

You should never have too bright a light directly overhead, either in the office or the bedroom, since this may cause health problems. It is a bad omen if a bulb blows in the office or bedroom whilst you are there. If the bulb is replaced immediately, all will be well. Have some spare bulbs handy for such an eventuality.

DRESSING TABLES SHOULD NOT FACE THE BED DIRECTLY

Never position your dressing table directly opposite the foot of your bed. The mirror itself will cause a great deal of bad luck, friction and relationship problems. If you cannot move your dressing table, keep all hand-mirrors, make-up and combs inside the drawers, and drape a cloth over the mirror. This temporarily solves the problem.

FIRE AT HEAVEN'S GATE

The northwest corner of any room or house
signifies heaven. Make sure that you do not
have a stove or a fireplace in this corner
since this signifies fire at heaven's gate. It is
regarded as very inauspicious by feng shui
masters.

FIRE AND WATER SHOULD NOT CLASH IN THE KITCHEN

The family stove or cooker should not be placed next to the sink or refrigerator. This creates a clash between water and fire elements, causing disharmony in the lives of the residents. Move the cooker (fire element) to the fire corner in the south of the kitchen to tap into the natural elements of the directions. Energizing the elements in this way brings good fortune to residents.

KEEP NINE GOLDFISH
FOR LUCK

A truly great way to activate excellent feng shui luck inside the home is to keep nine goldfish in an aquarium, eight red or golden and one black. If any of your fish die, do not worry, just replace them. It is said that if a fish dies it has absorbed the misfortune meant for a resident.

DISPLAY PEONIES FOR LOVE

The peony is the 'king of flowers', a symbol of good fortune associated with women and romance. Legend tells of Yang Kuei Fei, reputedly the most beautiful woman in Chinese history and concubine to the emperor. She kept him enthralled throughout her life and in homage to her he kept her bedchamber filled with peonies. It is believed that the peony keeps romance and love alive.

Grow Oranges
Or Limes

Bright red oranges signify gold because 'Kum', the Chinese word for oranges, also means gold. An orange or lime tree weighed down heavily with ripening fruit therefore symbolizes the ripening of good fortune and prosperity. Display them at the entrances to your home.

HANG COINS AND BELLS ON YOUR DOORS

Hang three Chinese coins (round with a square hole in the centre) tied with red thread on the inside door handles of your main doors. The red thread activates the essence of good fortune symbolized by the coins. On the outside hang bells, also tied with red thread. Never hang the bells or coins on the back door.

CACTI AND BONSAI
IN THE HOME

Avoid having prickly cactus plants inside the home. The thorns of these plants represent tiny arrows that cause killing energies to accumulate. Cacti can be placed outside the home for protection but bonsai plants, which represent artificially stunted growth, should not be displayed either inside or outside the home.

PROTECT THE FAMILY RICE URN

If you are a rice-eating household, keep your rice in a special urn and protect it because it symbolizes your family fortunes. Keep the urn hidden away and make sure that there is always rice in it so that you never see the bottom. If you wish, you can keep three coins tied with red thread inside a red packet at the bottom of the urn.

PLACE STEREO EQUIPMENT ON THE WEST WALL

All stereo and hi-fi equipment brings extra luck to the house when placed on the west wall of the living room. Stereo sets placed here create the potential for good fortune in the year 2003 and the following 20 years.

KEEP BROOMS AND MOPS
OUT OF SIGHT

Mops and brooms are associated with
sweeping out the negative and stale energy
of the home but they can also sweep away
good energy. Feng shui advises that you hide
them away after you have finished cleaning.

KEEP THINGS IN PAIRS

If you want someone to share your life with, surround your personal space with objects and ornaments in pairs, such as ducks, butterflies or birds.

TIPS FOR
THE BEDROOM

- Decorate the bedroom in red during the early years of a relationship. If red is too strong, use pink or peach. Red represents passion and strong yang energy and brings luck to those wanting children. Otherwise, use more muted yin colours.

- Never put plants or flowers in the bedroom but fruit is excellent, especially the pomegranate, a symbol of fertility.

- Hang paintings of children to symbolize descendants luck.

- Avoid anything that suggests water.

- Do not have a television facing the bed, and cover it when not in use.

- Hang a double happiness symbol.

HANG WINDCHIMES TO
INCREASE YOUR POPULARITY

To enhance your popularity, hang either a
two- or nine-rod windchime (crystal or
ceramic) in the southwest corner of your
living room. It is not a good idea to put one
in the bedroom. To enhance networking
luck, hang a metal windchime with six rods
in the northwest corner.

AVOID THREE IN
A PICTURE

It is believed in feng shui that three people
in a picture can lead to separation unless
they are closely related. Three friends in one
picture means that the one in the middle
will be separated from the two at either side.
This taboo does not apply to family
portraits.

TIPS ON HANGING FAMILY PORTRAITS IN THE HOME

Do not hang photographs of family members in the following places:

- Facing the toilet door
- Directly facing the front door
- Facing a staircase
- In the basement
- Directly under a toilet on the floor above

POINTING A FINGER CREATES BAD FENG SHUI

If someone points an index finger at you
while speaking to you, bad energy is directed
towards you. If you are subjected to too
much finger pointing, you will suffer. Tell
anyone who does this to stop. Likewise you
should not point at other people when
speaking to them, and never point scissors
or anything sharp at your friends.

Look Out For Heaven And Devil Men

Devil men are those who cause you heartache, harm you, or make you lose your temper. They are obnoxious and troublesome and should be avoided because they send negative energy your way.

Heaven men are usually helpful and kind and give you a guiding hand. Embrace them because they bring positive chi towards you.

NEVER USE CHIPPED GLASSES OR CROCKERY

You should never serve coffee or tea in a chipped cup, drinks in a chipped glass or pour from a jug with a broken rim. Drinking from a cup or glass which has even the tiniest flaw symbolically cuts the mouth or lip, affecting one's speech. Crockery or glass in the home that is chipped or broken should be thrown away immediately.

ALWAYS SAY NO TO
THE LAST PIECE

If you take the last piece of food on the plate
or the last portion of cake, or clean up left-
over morsels at the end of the meal, you are
supposedly creating poverty energies. Resist
that last mouthful.

TIPS ON SITTING

Never sit directly facing:

- The sharp edge of a table
- Open bookshelves that resemble blades
- A door or elevator
- A staircase
- A long narrow corridor
- A toilet door
- The edge of a square pillar

Never Sit At The Corner Of A Square Table

You should never sit at the corner of a square table, with the sharp edge pointed directly at you. If you are eating, you will not have a good meal. If you are playing a card game, you will lose. If you are with someone you want to impress, you will fail to do so. Shift your chair away from the corner.

Feng Shui For Your Desk

Leave the part of your desk directly in front of you empty of files, books and so on. Create the equivalent of a bright hall where good chi can accumulate. Piles of files should be higher to your left than to your right.

ITEMS ON
YOUR DESK

With a compass note the direction of each
corner of your desk, then place:

- Flowers in the east to attract good
  income luck
- A crystal paperweight in the southwest
  to create harmonious relationships
- A lamp in the south for good
  reputation luck
- Computer equipment in the west to
  strengthen your ability to cope under
  pressure

AUSPICIOUS
NUMBERS

The number 8 is widely regarded by the
Chinese as a lucky number, partly because
the word for 8 in Chinese sounds like
'growth and development'. This number also
represents future prosperity, particularly
between the years 2003 and 2023.
Nine is also lucky since it signifies the
fullness of heaven and earth. It is complete
and never changing.

BLOCK OUT EXCESSIVE SUNLIGHT

If you have a west-oriented office, you could suffer from too much sunlight and overwhelming yang energy. Block out excessive light with heavy curtains or blinds otherwise the yang energy will lead to quarrels and short tempers.

Good Feng
Shui Doors

Doors should always be solid; those with glass panels are not recommended.

- Doors with hinges are preferable to sliding doors.
- Doors should open inwards to be auspicious.

ENERGIZE THE FENG SHUI OF YOUR FILES

Energize all your important files with prosperity coins that symbolize good fortune. Activate these coins by tying them together with red ribbon. It is unnecessary to energize all your files, only the important ones.

DEVELOP A PROSPERITY SIGNATURE

A signature is said to attract great prosperity and success if it starts and ends with a firm upward stroke. Develop your own personal prosperity signature and practice it until it becomes second nature.

A Secret Feng Shui Ritual

Here's a secret feng shui tip a master gave me which I have used with great success. If you have a wish list, write it down on a piece of paper 49 times and sign your prosperity signature below it 49 times. Then burn the paper. Do this for 49 consecutive days. Your wish list will actualize.

NEVER HANG YOUR
WASHING OUT OVERNIGHT

Night energy is excessively yin so never hang
your washing out to dry after dark. Your
washing will absorb the yin energies of the
night and upset your feng shui. Also, it is not
advisable to bathe in water that has
absorbed the energies of the night. It is far
better to bathe in yang water.

Design An Auspicious Business Card

Design your corporate logo with care. Avoid designs that are too abstract or which are sharp, pointed or angular, especially if the points are aimed at your name. Use a dragon as the ultimate success symbol, but do not enclose it so that it cannot grow.

THE THREE-LEGGED FROG

One of the most effective prosperity boosters of symbolic feng shui is the three-legged frog. Place this wonderful creature anywhere in your living room to magnify your wealth luck.

INVITE THE GODS OF
WEALTH INTO YOUR HOME

The Chinese have several gods of wealth
which they display in their homes to attract
prosperity luck. My personal favourite is Tsai
Shen Yeh, who sits on a tiger. If he is difficult
to find, you could use Kuan Kung or the
three star gods, Fuk, Luk and Sau, all of
whom bring wealth and prosperity.

SPIRAL STAIRCASES ARE BAD NEWS

Spiral staircases are often designers' favourites but they are inauspicious in feng shui terms, particularly when located in the centre of the home. The spaces in between the steps cause money to drain away and the circular corkscrew shape unbalances the house. Spirals in the corner of a room are less harmful.

Square Pillars Often Cause Feng Shui Problems

Square, structural pillars directly facing an entrance should be covered with mirrors or other reflective material or softened with creeping plants. Round pillars are less harmful, particularly if they frame the front door, but if they face it they may cause similar problems.

SCREENS ARE EXCELLENT
FENG SHUI REMEDIES

As well as making superb room dividers, screens solve a multitude of feng shui problems associated with fast-moving, killing breath. Screens block, dissolve and dissipate bad energy (shar chi), but they must be placed in a straight line, either suspended from the ceiling or firmly attached to the ground. If placed in a zigzag fashion, shar chi will accumulate.

CREATE AUSPICIOUS COLOUR COMBINATIONS

SECTOR	DOMINANT COLOURS
South	red, orange
North	black, blue
East	green, brown
West	white, grey
Southeast	light green
Southwest	yellow, beige
Northeast	yellow, beige
Northwest	white, silver, gold

Different colours work best for different areas of the room.

SECONDARY COLOURS	COLOURS TO AVOID
yellow, green	black, blue
white, silver, gold	yellow, beige
black, blue	white, silver, gold
silver, gold, yellow	red, orange
light blue	grey white
red, orange	green, brown
red, orange	green, brown
grey, yellow	red, orange

CORRECT MISSING CORNERS

When corners representing wealth (southeast), relationships (southwest) or health (west) are missing, you will suffer acutely in these areas of your life. You can fill the missing corner by:

- Using a wall mirror to visually extend one wall

- Building an extension

- Installing a bright light there

TAKE CARE WHEN LOCATING YOUR COMPANY SIGNBOARD

Your corporate signboard must always be protected from bad feng shui. Place it high on your business premises and watch out for:

- Elevated highways and flyovers
- Communication masts and electricity pylons
- Elevated railway lines
- The sharp edges of nearby buildings

EARTH ENERGY BRINGS EXCELLENT FENG SHUI

If you want your business to benefit from earth energy, activate the three earth areas of your premises – the centre, and the southwest and northeast corners. Place large ceramic or pottery urns or crystal clusters in these places. Earth energy is strongest in the southwest corner.

USE MOTHER OF PEARL FOR ALL YOUR WOOD CORNERS

Enhance the energies of your wood element corners – the east and southeast – with mother of pearl to increase your turnover. The Chinese make mother of pearl furniture for this purpose and you should find some if you can.

TRIM YOUR PLANTS AND TREES REGULARLY

Trim your plants at least once every three weeks. Overgrown plants that look straggly and uncontrolled are not good feng shui. More importantly, you should trim your trees at least once a year. Always make certain that your trees do not overwhelm your home.

BE WARY OF PLANTS
WITH THORNS

Move all plants that have prickly thorns
away from the vicinity of your front door.
Thorny plants can create a protective energy,
but they should always be outside and not
too near the front door.

THROW OUT DRIED
LEAVES AND PLANTS

Dried, wilting or rotting plants emit large
doses of yin energy, with negative results.
Stale water, faded flowers and any dried
flowers should be removed from the house.
Be careful to do the same in the garden. This
will maintain the presence of healthy yang
energy.

A Door Flanked By Water Spells Tears

In your eagerness to introduce an auspicious water feature into your home, be careful. Too much water can spell danger. Never have water features (ponds, pools, fountains) on both sides of the front door.

DEVELOP SENSITIVITY TO YOUR IMMEDIATE SURROUNDINGS

Effective feng shui practice requires the ability to spot secret Poison arrows in the surrounding environment. These arrows hurt you only when they are pointed directly at your front door.

Deflect the killing energies created with a Pa Kua bought from Chinatown. Hang this protective yin symbol outside the house above the front door.

Some of the more obvious poison arrows are:

- A straight road
- A triangular roof line
- A high wall
- A large pillar
- A telephone pole
- A tree trunk
- The sharp corner of a building

MAKE YOUR MAIN DOOR AUSPICIOUS

Incorporate one or both of these auspicious features in your home to enhance the feng shui of your front door:

- Have a small water feature – an aquarium is best either on the left side of the door as you look out or directly facing it.
- Hang a bright light above the door – crystal if you can afford it – to welcome in the chi.

FENG SHUI ENERGIZERS
FOR STAIRCASES

Always keep the staircase and landing well lit to encourage the flow of chi. Hang a lucky painting on the landing or some auspicious calligraphy. If the staircase is too narrow, hang a large mirror to widen it.

LIVING ROOMS MUST HAVE AT LEAST ONE SOLID WALL

Have at least one wall without windows in your living room. This wall should ideally face the door into the room. This allows the chi to flow into and around the room instead of escaping through any windows directly opposite the door. In designing floor layouts, remember to let the chi move gently and slowly from one room to the next.

PLAY LOUD MUSIC
ONCE A WEEK

Clear your room with loud noise. In China,
the lunar New Year was celebrated loudly
with drums, cymbals and firecrackers to
wash out old energies and welcome in the
new. You can do the same with loud, happy
music. Play it for ten minutes – that's
enough.

THE WEALTH
VASE

Make a wealth vase and keep it hidden in
your cupboard. It can be made of gold,
crystal or glass. Fill it with semiprecious
stones and with soil taken from a rich man's
garden.

ABOUT THE AUTHOR

Lillian Too has written several bestselling books on Feng Shui, including *The Complete Illustrated Guide to Feng Shui*, *The Complete Illustrated Guide to Feng Shui for Gardens* and the *Feng Shui Fundamentals* series, also published by Element Books.

She heads the publishing and investment company that she founded in Malaysia, where she now lives. She is married with one daughter.

Lillian Too's website address is: www.lillian-too.com also check out: www.worldoffengshui.com – the first online Feng Shui magazine